A Bridge

Over

Troubled

Wall Street

Stephen Gardner

A Bridge Over Trouble Wall Street

By Stephen Gardner
Copyright © 2015, Stephen Gardner

ISBN- 13: 978-1512082739

MONEY IS BETTER THAN POVERTY,
IF ONLY FOR FINANCIAL REASONS.
WOODY ALLEN

A BRIDGE OVER TROUBLED WALL STREET

PRAISE FOR BRIDGE PLANS

I am an active real estate investor in New York City and Philadelphia. Being a Private Lender is a lucrative way to earn passive real estate income. Investing in Bridge Plans is an excellent way for investors to lock in high yields, while at the same time eliminating risk. Stephen explains in precise terms why every investor should look to diversify and incorporate this very safe and extremely lucrative strategy into their personal investment portfolio. It has made a world of difference for me.

Rick Kelly
New York and New Jersey

Stephen is the master of the safe money strategies. If you are looking for a place to grow your money at rates that exceed the rate of inflation and eliminates the risk associated with the stock market, then Stephen's strategy may be for you. This book will show you how to consistently get solid returns without tying up your money for long periods of time. As a former loan officer for ten years, this strategy not only makes sense to me, but is also one that gives my clients peace of mind.

Rod Ferrier
Virginia

Stephen Gardner has done it again! His ability to seek out and find creative ways for his clients to safely earn good returns is incredible. His ability to explain it in a simple and easy to understand format, is genius. By using a Bridge Plan, Stephen shows the everyday investor how to collectively leverage their money in commercial real estate to beat inflation and play in the same arena as the wealthiest people in America. You won't find Stephen on Wall Street and you won't find his clients there either. This book will show you how to use real assets to have a real future, a bright future, a predictable future.

Paul Parry
Mountaintop Insurance Solutions
Morgan, Utah

We are all looking for alternatives to the low interest rates at banks and the high risk of the Stock Market. Some investments are confusing and difficult to understand. Bridge Plans are not! Stephen does a great job of presenting this option in a clear and easy to understand formula. My clients have loved this strategy for replacing old CD's and for living off the interest.

Ken Feyer
Coral Springs, Florida

For my money and that of my clients, there's no safer and better investment than real estate. The Bridge Plan program allows you to invest in real estate the easy way. All the research and due diligence has been done for you by a team of experienced professionals with a long track record of success. Once again, Stephen Gardner does a masterful job of explaining how to take advantage of this simple yet safe way to earn real returns in a short, 12 month time frame. Say good bye to low earning savings accounts, CD's, bonds, and annuities. Why gamble in the stock market when investing in real assets is this easy and profitable? Thank you Stephen Gardner!

Morgen Jackson
Cocoa Beach, Florida

Bridges Plans allow you to invest in incoming producing commercial real estate without all the headaches. I have dealt in Bridge Plans for many years and have found them to be an excellent way to build real wealth. Stephen Gardner has again brought attention to an investment worthy of review. Bridge Plans are a great alternative to low interest rates offered by the bank. Here is the opportunity to partner with a super successful firm to have fractional ownership in properties you don't have to do the work on. Good returns inside of real assets is a formula for a successful future.

Ron Steiner Consulting
Mesa, Arizona

Stephen Gardner has a tremendous gift for teaching and he skillfully employs it here. Combine that gift with years of experience as a trusted financial advisor, in this book he presents solid, time-tested wisdom on how to safely and steadily grow wealth. Stephen gives many examples and experiences from actual clients, he also outlines key factors that every class of investor should carefully consider and understand: fees, the rule of 72, inflation, the terrible risk of Wall Street, and how saving with banks just doesn't cut it anymore. Every investor should understand this investment, and Stephen makes it easy to do so here, as he presents the Bridge Plan.

Paul F. Johnson
Salt Lake City, Utah

I've known Stephen for many years now as a client. His number one concern has always been protecting his clients' money and then growing it outside of Wall Street. His ability to find and present investments the public isn't aware is uncanny. Bridge plans will help clients earn a good rate of return using real estate, without all the hassle that comes with owning property. Using real estate gets back to the roots of what makes America great. This book will help you get back to the basics of managing your own money inside of real assets.

Devin Hubbard
Ogden, Utah

This book will open the eyes of many investors to a powerful and safe way to grow their money. A way to earn a competitive rate without all the risk of Wall Street. Thank you Stephen for taking the time to explain Bridge Plans in a way that is easy to understand.

Ron Weller
Dayspring Advisors Group, Michigan

.

DEDICATION

Thank you to Kacey, Gavin, Halle and Julia. You
are my inspiration and I love you.

Thank you to God for all of the good gifts that have
come into my life. I owe you everything!

Foreword

Stephen Gardner has done it again! As one of the premier authorities on safe money strategies, it always amazes me that Stephen continues to find opportunities for his clients to build wealth and security without touching the stock market.

In this book he's going to teach you a strategy that just may energize you again. It will remind you of the days when CDs were paying 5-6%. If you grasp this concept, it may have a major impact on the way you and other families will save for retirement. For those in retirement it will give you a way to live off your annual interest and leave your principal protected.

When I heard he would be writing his fourth book and it would be on bridge loans and first position commercial notes, I had no idea these assets were available to individual investors. We all know real estate can be a wealth builder, but it always came with either a high price tag or a ton of work to manage and maintain.

Now along comes an opportunity to own a fractional interest in a commercial property without the normal risks most investors face. I personally have owned interests in land, commercial buildings and real estate investment trusts. But with all of these, I was subject to additional expenses and taxes, and in most cases, a long time frame before I could either see a profit or recoup my money.

What if you could receive a profit from owning real estate without any of the downside AND you knew it could be done in only 12 months?

Stephen has researched this asset class extensively and now he is also going to give you one of the greatest gifts in life – hope.

Hope that you can now watch your retirement funds grow. Hope that you no longer have to look at your investment statements and see a loss. Hope that you can own a tangible asset that can grow your money short term like we used to see with CDs. Hope that you can go to sleep at night and know that regardless of what happens in the economy, the stock market, or at the bank, it won't affect this alternative investment.

We live in a turbulent world. Interest rates are down; inflation is silently eroding your investments and income; boomers are worried that they will become dependent on their children for assistance. Some are even concerned they will have to work until they die; or worse that they will outlive their money.

What if you could have a safe, simple and predictable investment that could eliminate all those issues? Those who have an open mind will see how it can have a major impact on the way they will save for both the short term and long term.

The days of working 37 years for the same company and retiring with a lifetime pension are gone. 401Ks and 403Bs are a way to save for the future, but may not be the safest way to do it. In fact, the only people getting rich from these plans are those who lure you into investing in them. What happened to the days of safe, guaranteed returns?

Stephen is going to pull back the curtain on how commercial investors have consistently grown their money using this strategy.

This investment is not for everybody. It's for those who want security, contractual growth, and need income.

Stephen gets it. He's spoken with hundreds of individuals who have these concerns and has steered them towards safety for themselves and their families.

From Stephen's in depth experience and his ability to cut through the clutter, he will provide you with a clear picture of what is going on in this industry.

Why you need to protect yourself first. Why now may not be the time to bet on the stock market if you want to retire comfortably.

It's time to stop accepting sub-optimal results in your portfolio, paying thousands of dollars in fees and worrying whether you will be offending your financial advisors. Ask yourself. Can you endure another 20-30% loss as you approach retirement? Will you be able to continue your lifestyle during retirement when the market drops again?

We know there are no perfect investments. Stephen does an incredible job of laying out the good and the bad to know whether investing in bridge loans may be a fit for you. That's one thing you can count on. It's your money and your decision. He just wants to make sure you have a clear picture of all the information before you decide. For most people this option will be new.

Stephen has a big heart and understands the principle of giving. I've never seen someone so passionate about helping others succeed, whether it's his advisors, clients, or prospects.

My prayer is you read this book with an open mind. It may be the one game changer you've been looking for to finally get peace of mind as you look to build and use your wealth. Fractional ownership in a short term commercial bridge loan may be right for you.

One more thought – take a minute and imagine where your money will be if you never have to worry about a loss again. Stop listening to the Wall Street propaganda and take control of your financial future. You'll be glad you did.

Mark Maiewski

Virginia's Leading College Planning Authority

PREFACE

After finishing my third book, I didn't think I would write another. Two of my books had become national best-sellers and the books were being used by over 400 wealth advisors nationwide.

As I started to look over my own finances, my wife and I talked about how we would like to be involved in real estate. We both know and have known many people that have made good money each year with real estate.

One of my Boy Scout leaders from my youth and later, as a boss during college, taught me the value of doing real estate. He and his family have successfully done over 300 Bridge Plans. They like the control and predictability they offer. Plus they could earn solid returns each year and not have to be committed to a property long-term. I also learned that more money could be made outside of the market and with less volatility. Investors only have to seek high returns from the market to make up for inevitable losses. If you remove the losses from the equation, the returns a Bridge Plan can provide will build a nice nest egg.

Wall Street is in trouble and banks are no help right now. We are 7 years from the last major stock market meltdown; a meltdown that took 30-50% of

Americans wealth with it. We have reached the top of the market again. Now would be a great time to pull your profits off the table and shift them away from Wall Street.

Before the invention of bridges, crossing the troubling and swift moving rivers of the world was dangerous. You may get across safely or you may be swept downstream. A bridge helped people safely get from where they were to where they wanted to be.

This book will be short and simple. One of my favorite aspects of a Bridge Plan is the simplicity of the program and its short time frame of 12 months. It makes being involved in real estate easy and enjoyable while at the same time giving investors the opportunity to make good returns.

If you are looking for a 500 page book that tells you all the hidden secrets of getting rich quick, this is the wrong book. There is nothing secret or complex here. Bridges plans get you back to the basics; using your hard earned money inside of real assets to make a good return year in and year out or just in a quick 12 month period.

This book will show you how to get from where you are now to where you want to be in the future with very little risk.

Chapter One

Undeserved Punishment

I'm going to tell you everything you need to know about the stock market: Nobody Knows Nothin'.

JACK BOGEL, Founder of Vanguard.

You are being punished! The American people are being punished, punished for an economic collapse you and I did not create. This punishment has to stop and we have the power make it happen.

On September 29th, 2008 the stock market slipped 777 points in a single day and caused an economic meltdown that created a global financial crisis. This large, single-day drop kicked off the greatest economic hardship since the Great

Depression.

When gambling, pulling a 7-7-7 is lucky and leads to great riches at the slot machines. For Americans and the rest of the world, 777 brought just the opposite. Most investors lost anywhere from 30-60% of their money in a very short period of time. For most, that 30-60% drop accounted for decades of saving.

This economic slip had come exactly 7 years to the month since the last major market correction in 2001. Many Americans were shocked. How could the stock market be taking so many people's hard-earned money away again? A decade's worth of savings were wiped out. Losses that surely crippled the American people more than they could even imagine. Later I will show you how devastating losing money really is and why the top investors in the world are obsessed with not losing money.

A banker is a fellow who lends you his umbrella when the sun is shining, but wants it back the minute it begins to rain.

MARK TWAIN

So how are you being punished today? You're being punished with low interest rates from the bank and risky investment options from Wall Street. For over 6 years now the Federal Reserve has kept interest rates the lowest they have ever been. Savings accounts that once earned 5% now only earn .1%. Checking accounts that used to pay 1-2% now charge more in fees than most people earn in interest each year.

These low interest rates are forcing us to either earn next to nothing on our hard-earned savings, or they are forcing our money back into the stock market where we risk losing again.

With how often the market loses, and the banks falling short of any chance of keeping up with inflation, your future sits on the edge of a financial cliff. You are being punished. Punished if you stay safe with a bank because your money simply isn't growing fast enough or punished by being forced back into the market where you risk losing large portions of your money.

Don't be fooled! The stock market is rigged and manipulated on a daily basis. Keep in mind the fact that we are 7 years out from the last economic meltdown. The stock market is setting new record highs all the time. To the inexperienced investor these record highs draw new investor dollars like a moth to a flame, but too many years of growth and all-time highs are seen as a red flag to the experienced investor.

The stock market cannot go up forever. Before the Great Depression, Americans thought they were rich. They thought nothing would change and they would continue to get richer and richer. This held true for a time. On paper they were rich until it all came crashing down.

Now fast forward to the year 2000. The technology boom witnessed major companies moving to the internet and investors believed growth would increase and continue on forever. Then the dot-com bubble burst and those investors experienced 3 years of back-to-back double digit losses. It was a devastating time.

Then 2008 hit and took back all the previous 6 years earnings and left America with what was later called the lost decade. Whatever money you had in 2000 was what most people had in 2010. 10 years without any real growth on your money. 10 years of interrupted compounding interest. It was probably a big blow to your self-esteem and an even bigger blow to your future. Now 7 years later, it seems the stage is being set again for another major collapse.

Your self-worth should never be tied to your net worth. However, in Teri and Michael's world the two seemed inseparable.

How could this be happening to us again they wondered? 2000-2002 had been a rough time. Teri and Michael's retirement accounts suffered major losses that they were just barely recovering from. 2009 was a rough year for many people. It had been an especially hard year for Teri and Michael. While on vacation in San Diego to celebrate Michael's retirement they got the phone call no one wants to get from their financial planner, the call that leaves a pit in your stomach.

Teri and Michael had just finished lunch at the Poseidon Restaurant. It was a warm spring day and they had been seated outside. They could see and hear the ocean waves rhythmically lapping the sand over and over again. It was only the first day of their week-long vacation, but it had been a good day.

Then the phone rang. It was Ben, their financial advisor. Teri could tell it was serious because Michael walked away from her and his posture sank. He eventually sat down on the sand and hung up the phone. He had just been informed that his retirement account was down 50% and he needed to decide what to do next.

I work with close to 500 families a year from all over the country and unfortunately this is a true story. In fact I've heard hundreds of similar stories. The Great Recession was now in full swing. Trillions of dollars were lost, decades of hard work and savings were wiped out and people were struggling just to stay employed. Can you still remember 2008? Can you still remember 2001?

There is a famous saying that rings all too true. "Those who fail to learn from history are doomed to repeat it."

Adding insult to injury

The average investor lost over 30% around 2008. It was a time most people will not forget. As one of my dentist clients told me, "It is a sting I still feel to this day."

What do you do after being told you've lost 30-60% of your wealth? Do you stick it out and hope it comes back? Do you put your entire life on hold? Do you switch back to the investments and savings strategies your parents and grandparents trusted? Most people just froze and let the stock market and banks determine their future.

For a large percentage of investors they simply switched to a cash position and desperately took whatever interest rate they could get. After all, it was better to earn small than lose again. To this day many people have still not gone back in to the stock market. Their money sits in CDs and Money Market accounts earning less than 1%. There is a better way, so keep reading.

TODAY'S INTEREST RATES	DATA PROVIDED BY Bankrate
Mortgage Equity Savings Auto Credit Cards	
5 yr CD	1.49%
2 yr CD	0.82%
1 yr CD	0.67%
MMA $10K+	0.33%
MMA $50K+	0.54%
MMA Savings	0.38%
MMA Savings Jumbo	0.46%
National averages from Bankrate.com	

After the worst financial calamity since the Great Depression, the Federal Reserve dropped interest rates down to practically nothing. The savings accounts that were earning 5% vanished. The CDs that were paying 6-8% finished out their cycle and then dropped down to nothing. As of this writing the largest bank in Utah has a 12 month CD earning .4%. Yep 4/10th's of one percent! The best online CD is paying .67% according to Bankrate.com.

A bank is an institution that will lend you money if you can prove you don't need it.

BOB HOPE

Yet some people are still earning 5-7% interest annually with very little risk and with short 12-18 month time frames. They are not investing in the stock market and they are not investing at the bank. They have gone private and it's made all the difference. Investors have found control and predictability!

Chapter Two

Please Don't Think

Remember the golden rule: he who has the gold makes the rules.

UNKNOWN

Your bank is in the business of making money, big money in fact! As the board of directors meets each month, the pressing topic is always how do we make more money. It's never how do we make our clients more money. You see, the bank only needs you so they can leverage your money; so they can lend it to someone else at a higher rate and produce profits. When you understand money, you realize the bank needs you much more than you need the bank. We have to think like a bank in order to earn like a bank.

Banks don't care what you are earning, only that they are earning more than you and that you are earning just enough to leave your money with them. They dangle a carrot just enticing enough that you never leave the treadmill. People confuse activity with progress and the banks use this to their advantage. We somehow feel that having our money with the nice lady at the bank makes us safe and that it is growing at the best rate they can offer. Is the money you have at the bank really growing? Is your money really safe?

Since 2008, 465 banks have failed and closed their doors. Most banks offer their customers FDIC insurance to make them feel cozy and safe. However, the FDIC recently admitted to only having 1.15% in reserves for all the money banks have on deposit. Out of 100% they have promised to protect, they only have 1.15%. This leaves money at the bank vulnerable to the next market crash.

> *We are fast approaching the stage of the ultimate inversion: the stage where the Government is free to do anything it pleases, while the citizen may act only by permission.*

AYN RAND

The Federal Reserve has lowered interest rates for the public to nearly zero in an attempt to make banks financially strong again. This is hurting the middle class and most Americans. This policy is only benefiting the banks. You and I are too small for bailouts and too small to benefit from good rates. Here are a few reasons why lending is more difficult and interest rates are so low.

1. Banks lend to each other using something called LIBOR. It's the rate at which banks lend to each other to make additional interest on idle reserves. This rate has been slashed and as a result, banks aren't able to lend as freely to each other as they once did.

2. The Fed has made lending requirements extremely difficult. This has forced banks to clean up the old loans they already had but makes it difficult to lend out new money. This leads to a stagnant economy.

3. The Fed has banks placing their reserve funds in the Feds account. Basically they are paying banks a high enough rate with no risk to place their money with the Fed versus putting it into a working economy. Banks have incentive to place excess money with the Fed but not to lend it to individuals or businesses.

This leads to low interest rates, a slower economy and Americans not getting the growth they need on their money. Your money may be safe at the bank, but it is safely losing buying power.

More will be covered on this subject in the chapter on how inflation erodes your money and steals your future.

Banks don't want you to know about the many other ways you can grow your money. They don't want you to take control of your money. They want you to be completely and totally dependent upon them. If they educate you too much they run the risk of creating competitors and losing clients. This is not a good business model for them and so most people are left in the dark earning nothing. The question then becomes, are you going to sit and continue to take the abuse or are you committed to finding a better way?

Don't feel bad for the banks, they aren't hurting right now. Most banks are having their best growth years ever. Thanks to real estate, bank owned life insurance plans and fractional trusts, most banks are earning 5-14% with little to no risk. But, don't expect any of that to be passed on to you or me. We must find our own investments and take control of our own money. This book will share a few insights that the wealthy use to take control of their money and earn 5-7% with little to no risk, while doing so in short 12 month time frames.

Banks would suffer tremendously if you knew how to buy silver. Banks don't want you knowing about annuities and real estate. Banks don't want you to find out about the safety and tax benefits of properly structured life insurance or fractional trusts and they certainly don't want you knowing about bridge plans and hard money lending. In fact, they just want you to rely on them completely and not ask questions.

If a bank can get you to stop thinking for yourself and be dependent upon them, they know they will have access to your money for life. America has been outsourcing their money and investments to the big banks and Wall Street for far too long. We are all more capable and intelligent than we give ourselves credit. With a little education and the right opportunity you could be earning 5% or more while the bank pays .5%. That is 10 times the difference in what you could be earning and this book will show you how. It's time to take personal responsibility for our lives, our money and our retirement.

Chapter Three

Personal Responsibility

We have met the enemy, and he is us.

POGO

I am constantly trying to teach my children that taking personal responsibility for their lives and actions will make them happier. If you have no one to blame but yourself, you will be happier.

Even when things go wrong, taking responsibility helps resolve matters faster. Do you take responsibility with your money or is someone else to blame for your losses or poor interest rates?

Taking responsibility for your money will earn you more money. Being more involved in your money will earn you more money. What you focus on grows.

> *The best way to predict the future is to invent it.*

ALAN KAY

The majority of my clients are millionaires and multi-millionaires, and let me tell you they think differently than most people. We can gain insight from how they think and use it to our advantage. Success leaves clues.

> *I find it fascinating that most people plan their vacations with better care than they plan their lives. Perhaps that is because escape is easier than change.*

JIM ROHN

For starters, the wealthy refuse to settle for low interest rates. They search out, research and find ways to make better returns on their money. They are hypersensitive when it comes to losing money, but they also know they must beat inflation.

The wealthy are always working to improve their savings rate. They do this in two ways. Number one, they don't depend on interest rate to get them to their goals. They know that what they contribute matters more than what they earn and that is something they can control. It doesn't matter if you can earn a 15% return if you have no money set aside.

So what can you do to increase the amount of money you are saving and contributing to your future? The best way is to get on an automatic savings plan. If your goal is to save 15% of everything you make, then have it automatically drafted out of your checking account every month. Remember the saying "out of sight, out of mind." We don't spend what we don't think we have. So make it automatic and save as much as you can. Chapter 6 will show you where to safely grow your money each year.

Number two, once the wealthy have a system for saving they look to make sure they are getting the best interest rate. Inflation tends to rise at around 3% each year, so this is the number they have to beat in order to maintain and grow their future buying power. More will be discussed on why beating inflation is so imperative in the next chapter.

Can you honestly say you understand the stock market, futures, mutual funds and other risky investments? Becoming familiar with how your investments really work is crucial. Here are some simple questions to ask yourself about your investments:

1. Do I understand how my investments really work?
2. Could I explain it to someone else and have them understand it?
3. Can I do the math to see how my money will grow?
4. Do I have a contractual growth rate or am I just hoping for the best?
5. How do fees and commissions affect my money and how it will grow over time?
6. What is my exit strategy for getting out of this investment? Or what is my time commitment with this investment?

Hope is a wonderful attribute, but a terrible investment strategy. Most people are using hope as the key driver for their future. Heck, most investment advisors use hope as a strategy because they have no control over the stock market. They say, "based on history this should give you a 7% return." SHOULD! SHOULD! What ever happened to having a contractual interest rate?

Would you rather have a contract that dictates how your money will grow or leave it to luck? Most would rather know how their money will grow, but this isn't the way investing works these days. This puts too much pressure and responsibility on companies to perform. It would be better for them if in the small print, the companies were excused from any losses or guarantees. That way, the investor is to blame when things go wrong.

The man on top of the mountain didn't fall there.

VINCE LOMBARDI

This isn't how we run my practice. For my clients, products are used that have guarantees and that have safety at their heart. Most of all, investment strategies are used that have a contract in place for how your money will grow, a legally-binding contract that obligates the company to pay you what it has promised.

One last thing the wealthy do that can benefit most people is to decide to be wealthy. This decision forces their mind to look for opportunities and not settle for mediocre returns. This decision gives them incentive to work hard for their families and to be good savers. Most people don't save like they should these days. They expect interest to do all the work and never focus on adding enough principle to their account. With interest rates between .1-.4% you can see why many people are spending their money versus saving it.

A client of mine is in the oil and gas business.

She is very sharp and earns a good living. After setting up her investments and showing her how her money will grow, she started dedicating herself to saving more. She said, "I finally have a place to confidently grow my money and now I want to save and see it grow each and every year."

By taking responsibility for your money you are where the buck stops. You are to blame if you aren't where you want to be, but when things go right, you will also have the pleasure of knowing you are where you are because of your efforts. You can be self-made and you can be the reason behind your own success. I wish this kind of success for you and I know the strategy in this book will help you get there.

Chapter Four

Escaping Inflation

Can anybody remember when the times were not hard and money not scarce?

RALPH WALDO EMERSON

I don't think it is any secret that life in America is expensive. The prices for goods and services are constantly rising. I remember my grandmother telling me how a cheeseburger used to cost $.15 and how a coke was a nickel. Nowadays, you can't get a decent combo meal for less than $6 unless you like eating off the dollar menu.

This increase in prices over time is inflation. Inflation is one of the few things that rarely stops increasing and if we aren't aware of it, we may soon find we don't have the money we need to live on. We must beat this enemy of wealth or it will crush us.

Inflation seems to run at about 3% annually, according to our government. Of course, this doesn't take into account food or gasoline prices. In the last chapter, I mentioned how beating inflation is imperative. If your money isn't keeping up with the rising cost of living, pretty soon you may find yourself without enough money to afford the lifestyle you have grown accustomed to.

Do you know the Rule of 72? This is an important rule and one you should be using to measure the growth of your money. Basically, you divide 72 by the interest your money is earning to determine how often your money will double. This formula can also be used with inflation to determine how expensive things will be in the future.

Let's start with the bad news and see how expensive it will be to live in the future by measuring the effects of inflation. If we take 72 divided by 3% we get 24 years. That means that a $3 loaf of bread will cost $6 per loaf 24 years from now. A $20 haircut will cost $40. A $200,000 house will cost $400,000. You've probably seen this in your lifetime.

When I first started driving, gas was $.95 a gallon. In 2014 gas was $3.53 a gallon. When I was a kid, movies were just $3 a ticket. Now it is closer to $9 and if you live on either of the coasts, it is closer to $12 a ticket. What has changed the most in your lifetime from when you were a kid until today? Cars, houses, food.

A family friend of mine from the baby-boomer generation was shocked by how much a mortgage cost these days. When he owned a house at my age, his payment was $315 a month. Now you can barely buy a decent car with that monthly car payment.

Inflation is constantly working against us. It doesn't sleep and it is no respecter of persons. It just silently increases every year. Since it is constantly working against us year-in and year-out, we have to make sure our money is growing faster than inflation. With bank rates as low as they are, this hasn't happened in over 6 years. In fact, CD rates have not been above 5% since the year 2000. This demonstrates 15 years of poor growth opportunity with the banks.

Let's see an example of how money can grow in our favor. If you are able to earn 6% annually, your money will double every 12 years. 72 divided by 6 is 12. This means if you have $100,000 today earning 6%, that original $100,000 will grow to $200,000 12 years from now. This is important to know!

Interest rate	Years to double
5%	14.4
6%	12
7%	10.28
8%	9
10%	7.2
12%	6

Now imagine you are Scott who lives in Salt Lake City, Utah. You have $200,000 earning .25% at the bank. If we apply the rule of 72, Scott won't see his money double for 288 years! Or maybe you are James in New York with $350,000 earning .5%. It will take 144 years for his money to double! With inflation at 3% his money is falling behind by 2.5% compounded annually.

Interest works for you. It isn't just to get you to your retirement goals. It is to get you through retirement as the price of everything continues to increase.

One last example. This makes me furious at the Federal Reserve and the banks because it seems criminal to me. I met with a woman in her early 70's last year. She had saved for years and was able to squirrel away $200,000 in mutual funds before she retired. At the time, her savings were earning 5.5% with ING Direct and her plan was to move the money from the stock market to the savings account so she could live off the interest as a way of supplementing her social security income.

A year after retiring she still had not moved the money away from the market because it was doing so well. It seemed foolish to pull out when the market was so hot. She ended 2008 with around $110,000 in her mutual funds. That $90,000 loss was equivalent to over 10 years of savings, lost in less than a year! This was money she would need to live on the rest of her life. She was kicking herself for not pulling out when her gut told her to do so. Eventually she did pull out because she didn't know if the markets would rise or fall.

By the time she moved her money to her savings account, it was only earning .30%. She could now look forward to an insulting $27.50 a month in interest to help supplement her retirement. It is hard to sit across from someone and hear that story and not wish you had met a few years earlier.

To look someone in the eyes as they divulge the reality of their current circumstances is humbling. I wished I had met her before she lost $90,000. My heart ached for this woman who, because her spouse passed away many years earlier, was now going it alone and with less money than she had planned, while earning less interest than she could have ever imagined.

We were able to get her into a bridge plan that was earning 6% and would pay her monthly interest. With this plan she was now able to receive $550.00 a month in interest to help supplement her income needs; money that will come to her directly every month. Money she can count on. $550.00 a month compared to $27.50 a month is a huge difference- a 1900% increase in her monthly interest, especially on her fixed income. The extra $522.50 we were able to get her made the difference between making it or not. She now has the peace of mind that she won't run out of money, she won't become a financial burden on her children and she won't have to eat into her principal to survive.

Don't permit low interest rates and inflation to rob you of a great retirement. There are solutions, but the bank does not seem to be one of them. Perhaps that will change, but if you are not keeping up with inflation we need to look at other options for your money and fast.

Chapter Five

True Cost of Losing

Safety doesn't happen by accident.

FLORIDA HIGHWAY SIGN

Losses at any time are not good. It's terrible to lose money during retirement age or as you are building towards retirement. It can cost you even more over your lifetime when you suffer losses at a young age.

Let's say that you are 45 years old and you lose $50,000 in the stock market. Let's assume you could have averaged 7% on that $50,000 over the next 20 years until age 65. That $50,000 loss really cost you $193,000. $50,000 compounding at 7% for 20 years would have grown to $193,000. Isn't that terrible? From age 45 to 65, you lost $193,000 that you could have had thanks to earned interest. That is $193,000 which would definitely come in handy during retirement but instead benefited someone else's account.

Many people get confused and think, "Oh well, my money came back. Now I'm back to where I was before the crash." That thinking is a fallacy for two reasons.

Number one, did you continue to contribute to your retirement account? Often if you own a 401K, you have continued to make contributions. Part of that growth is not growth at all. It is just additional principal payments that you added to your own account.

Secondly, your money does not come back. It never just reappears. Nobody deposits it back into your account. In actuality, your money has to grow back to the point where it was before you lost it. You have to re-earn that money. In the case of those that lost money in 2007 and 2008, it took 5.5 years for the stock market to get back to break even. In the case of the NASDAQ, it took 15 years just to break even from its drop in 2000. Can you imagine waiting 15 years to get your money back?

Somehow we feel better saying, "Oh, I got my money back." The more appropriate way to think is "Where would my money be today if I hadn't lost in the first place?" If you have ever lost money in the stock market this can be a haunting question, one perhaps you don't really want to know the answer to.

Let's continue with the above example and say you will live 20 years in retirement. Now, that $50,000 loss didn't just cost you $50,000 or $193,000. The amount could actually be $748,000. $50,000 compounding at 7% for 40 years is $748,000. Isn't that shocking? ONE $50,000 loss at age 45 could cost you three quarters of a million dollars over your lifetime. Wall Street doesn't want you to think like this. Otherwise, investors would run for the hills.

I don't gamble, because winning $100 doesn't give me great pleasure. But losing $100 pisses me off.

ALEX TREBEK, host of Jeopardy!

This is why Warren Buffet has two rules for investing. The first is, "Never lose money." Rule number two is, "Never forget rule number one." Yet, this is exactly what Wall Street wants you to believe, that it's okay to lose money while you're young because, "Oh, it's going to come back." News flash, it never comes back! You contribute more, and you earn new interest, but you never get your money back. Worse, you lose the time and the money you should have accumulated had you continued compounding your money.

World famous speaker and author, Tony Robbins recently interviewed the top 50 wealthiest investors in the world, people like Warren Buffett, Ray Dalio and Charles Schwab. The insight he gained on investing from these titans of finances was amazing, but he said the most common thread among them was their obsession over not losing money. They would rather not earn than lose money because of how much effort and time is required to make up for losses.

You can be young without money, but you can't be old without it.

TENNESSEE WILLIAMS

The older we get the more important it is to avoid major setbacks in our retirement accounts. Most people simply don't have time to recover from market losses. Owning an asset that is not correlated to the stock market gives you peace of mind and provides uninterrupted growth on your retirement account.

So how does interrupted growth affect your retirement account? Let's say you have $100 and you lose 50%. You now have $50. Let's say tomorrow you get 50% back. Now how much do you have? Most people are inclined to say $100, but you actually only have $75.

You see, the 50% you earned the next day is on your new, lower amount of $50. You would actually need a 100% return just to get back to break even on the original $100 you started with. That's why a drop in the market hurts for such a long time. It can take 5 to 10 years to claw back to where your account values were prior to taking a loss.

Market loss can cost you decades of savings and time, plus leave you needing much larger returns to get back to break even. Let me illustrate in the table below what is needed to make up for a different percentages of loss.

Percent needed to get back to break even after a market loss:

Percent Lost	Percent needed to break even
-20%	**25%**
-30%	**43%**
-40%	**67%**
-50%	**100%**
-60%	**150%**
-70%	**233%**

My favorite things in life don't cost any money. It's really clear that the most precious resource we all have is time.

STEVE JOBS

The table above makes it very easy to see why it took 5.5 years for the S&P 500 to climb back to break even after losing in 2007 and 2008. I know it seems crazy to show a 70% loss in the table, but from 2007 until the market hit bottom the stock market experienced a 52% total drop. During the

Great Depression the stock market dropped by 89% and took 22 years to recover from the losses.

Losing money wreaks havoc on your accounts and steals the time your account needs to compound your money. The interruption caused by losses can rob you of hundreds of thousands of dollars in retirement. On average, the markets drop every 5 to 7 years. It can then take 5 to 7 years to break even. Sometimes the market breaks even just in time to lose again.

We saw this in 1987, 1994, 2001, and 2008. There is a definite pattern to be seen. If history holds true 2015-2016 could be a rough time to be gambling in the markets. We know the market cannot go up forever. The scary part is we never know when it will drop or how fast. No one ever says, "I saw the market dropping and just let it happen to me." It is too unpredictable and gives little control to investors.

I am not ashamed to admit that I was one of the people that lost money in my own 401k. I ended up losing almost half of my money in 2008. Years of hard work and discipline were taken from me in a single year. That gut-wrenching incident is what started my crucial journey to learn strategies to safely grow money outside of Wall Street.

To this day I have never lost any of my client's money. I credit this with where I recommend they grow their investment dollars. It is paramount that your money be safe and that you earn a solid contractual return each year.

Chapter Six

Problem Solved

To become financially independent you must turn part of your income into capital; turn capital into enterprise; turn enterprise into profit; turn profit into investment; and turn investment into financial independence.

JIM ROHN

The task ahead would be difficult, if not impossible to complete. It had never been done and yet it had to be done for the future progress of America. A bridge had to be built for trains to cross the grand Mississippi River.

Up to this point no one had built a bridge across the wide Mississippi River that could support the weight of a train. This bridge would have to be different. It could not be like the other attempts that would *look* stable and sure, but would then collapse as a train crossed. Poorly built train bridges had been the cause for hundreds of deaths in the 1860's. If America was to grow and have any kind of future, the East and the West had to be connected and the Eads Bridge would be the solution.

In order to get the bridge built, a young Andrew Carnegie, soon to be the richest man in the world, was hired to produce and supply the steel. At the time no one had heard of steel bridges and even fewer trusted the idea. It would either be the great engineering feat of its time, or it would be the cause of a terrible calamity. The Eads Bridge was the first steel bridge and was the longest arch bridge in the world.

Upon completion of the Eads Bridge in 1874 a connection between the East and West coast was created. The bridge was finished and beautiful. However, there was one problem. No one trusted the bridge or the steel that held it up, so no one would use the bridge or send a train over it.

At the time there was a theory that an elephant, a very wise and cautious animal, would not cross over unsteady ground because they could feel it in its feet. Eads and Carnegie hired John

Robison, a circus owner with an elephant, to host a parade for the town to cross the bridge behind the elephant. The day came and the town waited with anticipation. The elephant walked up to the bridge and stopped. It studied the bridge for a long time. Could this bridge solve the town's problems? Could this bridge bring the money and the new business their town needed to survive?

The elephant placed one foot on the bridge and then another. Soon after, the elephant successfully crossed the 6,442 foot-long bridge. The people cheered and their hearts were filled with courage. Finally, they could trust in the bridge's plan and the country could grow and expand.

I share this story with you because it illustrates a few points. We are at a time when America is in need of creative solutions to grow. Jobs are down. Income is down. Interest rates are low and stock market risk is high. This combination could lead to another great recession.

I learned from a wise CEO many years ago, never to approach him with a problem without being ready to provide a solution. Just pointing out the problem didn't help. An action plan was needed.

In the case of low interest rates and high stock market risk, the solution is a bridge plan.

A bridge plan is fractional ownership in commercial bridge loans to business owners that need short-term lending to complete or start a project. To many, this may be a new type of saving and investing, but it has been around for many years. Some call it peer to peer lending, personal loans or hard money lending.

You cannot survive earning low interest rates. You will outlive your money and the world around you will become too expensive. Your money's buying power must keep up with the rising cost of living or you will be left behind.

For many seniors and baby boomers, outliving their money or becoming a financial burden on their adult children is their number one concern. For over six years now, the Federal Reserve has forced low interest rates on us. This was good if you wanted to buy a home, but for the rest of America it has been detrimental and damaging.

> *I have enough money to retire comfortably for the rest of my life. Problem is, I have to die next week.*

ANONYMOUS

Low interest rates are forcing investors back into the stock market for any chance of beating inflation. The dilemma then becomes, do I risk losing to inflation or losing to market loss. Both are inevitable and both are guaranteed. No market rises forever and inflation never sleeps. So what do we do?

We must beat inflation, but we don't have to take unnecessary risks in investments we can't understand or control. Control and predictability are crucial.

> *When I was young, I thought that money was the most important thing in life; now that I am old, I know that it is.*

OSCAR WILDE

A bridge plan provides both control and predictability in an easy to understand investment that has several layers of built in protection. A bridge plan is a winning combination of safety, security and convenience for those involved.

A bridge plan allows investors to collectively pool their money together to provide a lump sum of capital to businesses that are looking to expand or improve upon their income generating properties.

Imagine a commercial office space owner needing to expand and build out space he or she is ready to lease. They have good cash flow and their clients are happy, so they want to expand. They find a business that wants to lease from them and needs new space built so they can successfully grow their business.

The building owner will need a lump sum of money to start and complete the project. They have good cash flow but need a larger amount of money up front to start construction. The completed project will bring added revenue and monthly cash flow so they look for a short-term, 12 month bridge loan to complete the upgrades.

With tighter lending restrictions, banks have made it difficult for business owners to get the capital needed to grow. Banks would much rather lend to someone that already has an existing loan or to a building owner who can prove increased value of the building using a professional appraisal done by the bank. This difficult lending environment is a business owner's problem and our group's opportunity to provide a solution.

When such opportunities come along, our investors have the ability to pool their money for a short term loan and make a solid rate of return. By cutting out the bank and filling the role of lender, we earn the higher return and have control over which properties we lend on.

This is a great solution to the building owner because 12 months of higher interest in exchange for the ability to complete their project and increase their monthly cash flow, is it worth it. Once completed, the building owner will have the building appraised and the loan refinanced to a lower rate with the bank. The building owner may even sell off the property for a profit. We help them bridge the gap for 12 months.

Bridge plans provide needed capital on worthy projects. These projects provide jobs and income to families as well as improve our buildings and landscape. Our investors also benefit from higher returns as well.

I recently worked with a Florida couple in their 80's, who had been earning .3% on their money for the last 6 years. As the price of goods and services has increased, so had this couples need to supplement their social security income each month. Ideally they needed to have $2,000 extra per month. They did not want to eat into their principal in case they needed it down the road. They also knew they could not survive on what the banks were offering.

As the husband explained to me, "I don't want to go back into the stock market. Before the market dropped I had enough money to take care of myself and live off the interest comfortably. I lost close to half of our money when the stock market dropped in 2008. It caught us off guard and we were not prepared. We are paying for it now with less money and the low interest rates."

The couple had saved and invested wisely up until 2008. They had passed on trips and lived below their means so they could save. Then in a years' time, half of their hard work and savings was taken. At the time we met, he had $400,000 sitting at the bank. He was roughly earning $100 a month in interest. These low rates had forced him to start living off the principal to make up for the difference his social security and bank interest failed to provide.

I was able to introduce him to the bridge plan program. He had always wanted to be involved in real estate, but didn't want the work that came along with owning multiple properties. Up to this point he had never considered lending his own money to others in return for interest. He had always let the bank or stock market have that opportunity with his money.

After a couple weeks of researching the program and the companies involved he and his wife decided to move forward. We were able to lock a 7% guaranteed return for him and give him flexibility to take out a portion or all of his principal every 12 months. This solution provided him with $28,000 a year in interest or $2,333.33 in monthly interest payments that were mailed to his home every single month.

This man could have stayed with the bank and earned $100 a month; the same bank that would have taken his money and prudently lent it out in real estate to someone else. Or he could act like the bank and become the lender and earn $2,333 a month. If this were you, what would you choose?

- Every commercial opportunity is weighed out and researched.
- Each property has two appraisals done to make sure the building values are correct.
- A building can have no other liens or delinquent taxes.
- Our investors must be able to assume the first position on the lien
- Our group always takes a second position.

There is nothing like having the group you invest with, place their own skin in the game with you. This happens on every Bridge Plan.

In addition to a title search, lien search and

double appraisals, the group will only lend up to 65% of the value of a building and usually they stay under that. This means that if a building is worth $1,000,000 the most the group would ever lend would be $650,000. This allows for the building's value to change during the course of the 12-month loan, but not put our investors' money at risk.

In the event that a loan does default, the group has a large reserve account to draw upon. Would it give you peace of mind to know the group has never missed a payment or defaulted? Plus, it is written in their contract that they guarantee the rate and the principal protection for the investor. By collectively pooling your money with other investors and partnering with an experienced company, the outcome and results are incredible.

A doctor's plan adjustment

Last autumn I was working with a chiropractor on her tax planning. In the course of our discussion she mentioned that she owned her own building and had an old IRA that was just sitting stagnant. In fact, she said it had not grown in the last 5 years. The fees were equal to the low growth the account was experiencing, but she didn't know where else to grow it.

After wrapping up her tax-free plan, I again brought up the IRA account she had mentioned some weeks earlier because I was concerned how it wasn't growing. I introduced her to the bridge plan and I went over how it would work for her. She was fascinated by the whole concept. As someone that owned a building, she understood the need for capital and could understand how a short bridge loan for 12 months could help her increase the building's value or add increased cash flow each month. It actually gave her some future ideas for her own building.

We started by moving the IRA over into a bridge loan for a shopping center near Los Angeles, California. It was a 12-month project that would earn her 5.75% for the year. To go from no growth to 5.75% was a huge increase for her. She knew she needed that money to grow, but when you are running multiple businesses it is hard to even come up for air sometimes.

Her plan now is to save $1,000 a month in her account. Each 12 months as her principal with the group is released, we will add to her account and roll the principal and earnings, along with the newly saved money into the next property. She will now, for the first time, experience uninterrupted compounding growth on her money.

The group has helped all kinds of businesses get the capital they need to grow and update their properties. We have helped commercial buildings, multi-unit apartment complexes, condominiums, mixed use space, shopping malls, single-family rental units, high-end luxury wedding spaces, ski resorts, hotels, beach resorts, water-bottling plants and the list goes on. The key is to make sure the building appraises well and the borrower has healthy cash flow.

Our money can then go to work in their opportunity and this provides us with better-than-bank returns. To this day the Eads Bridge still provides a passageway for trains and cars. The bridge opened up a whole new world of opportunity for that town and our country. Bridge plans will open up a whole world of opportunity for you as well.

Chapter Seven

Understanding Bridge Plans

If you depend on your company to take care of your retirement, your future income will be divided by five. Take care of it yourself, and you can multiply your future income by five.

JIM ROHN

I want to share a powerful concept that was shared with me many years ago by a very successful multi-millionaire. He taught me that most of the big money-makers and successful investors, have figured out how to make money with OPM and OPO.

OPM - Other People's Money

OPO - Others People's Opportunities

Banks are top of the line pros when it comes to making money using other people's money. Maybe you have a loan or money at the bank right now or have had in the past. Let's say I have a saving account earning .3% or a CD earning .6%, but I also have a car loan with the same bank at 5% interest. The bank takes in my money at .3% and charges me 5% to take it out. That is a 4.7% marginal spread that the bank is making off my money.

In the case of a bridge loan, a company may borrow $1 million from us at 10% interest, but they can do the upgrades and sell the building for $1.5 million. They would pay $100,000 in interest and still make $400,000 in profit. We are happy and so are they. It's a win-win situation. We took advantage of their skill set and opportunity and they took advantage of our money to complete a project.

Cash flow versus lump sum

The reason we use bridge plans and the reason companies use our money comes down to a supply and demand opportunity. Our group collectively offers a lump sum; money that is needed now to start construction, buy materials, pay workers and improve or build out a property. These companies need our lump sum to get going.

We are the OPM in the equation and our lump sum opens the door.

The borrower is the OPO and as a group, we want their healthy cash flow. The borrower has the ability to make monthly payments, knowing that the improvements will lead to a profit or increased monthly cash flow. We see them as a way to keep money coming in on a monthly basis in exchange for our lump sum. We are willing to make the loan, so long as they are willing to compensate us for money they need.

This is good business and the sign of a healthy economy. Thanks to tight lending restrictions, our economy doesn't have money flowing like it needs to. This leads to low interest rates and stagnant money at the bank.

Opportunity is a powerful motivator. The word opportunity is an old shipping word. According to many sources on the origin of the word, it originated in the 14th century when seaside communities had only a few ports available for merchant ships to dock and exchange their goods with the town. When a ship would leave, there would be an open port for the next ship to slip in and sell their goods and wares. Open-port-unity became the word that was used. Nowadays we say, "when opportunity knocks, you answer."

New construction, commercial leasing and company expansion opens ports or opportunities to slip in and make money. With bridge plans, we are looking for the right opportunities to lend our money and make a good return. It's a good business to be in and a great place to put your money to work for yourself, others and our economy.

Characteristics of an ideal investment

I'd like to share a few reasons why I believe a bridge plan is an ideal and safe investment.

Performance:

Take a minute and think about the wealthiest people you know. Do they own real estate? 99% of the time my clients answer of course they do. Why would they choose to have real estate in their portfolio? Real estate is one of the best places to grow money.

As one of my wealthier clients who owns significant real estate pointed out, "last I checked God isn't making any more land." Real estate opens up a multitude of opportunities. Buying and flipping real estate is a very good way to make money.

According to Forbes Magazine's Billionaire Report, real estate is the 3rd most common way people became billionaires. Many of the billionaires listed own 10 or more properties. Most don't own any property directly but the money they have lent is backed by real estate.

Don't confuse this with owning your primary residence. I believe parking money in your house is a terrible idea. Your equity only appreciates by 1-2% annually and it is locked up unless you sell or finance it out. Think about this--a house will gain or lose value whether you have equity in it or not. Have you known anyone that fell on hard times like a job loss or the great recession and they couldn't access their equity? Using your house as a bank is a surefire way to lose the inflation battle. Using your house as an ATM is even worse.

The performance I am talking about is the opportunity of income producing real estate. Rental income. Office space leasing. Land development. This is where the money is, but it is also where a lot of the work is. With a bridge plan you are putting up the money. You're not collecting rent, paying insurance, dealing with maintenance issues, paying interest, closing costs, remodel and upkeep costs, or loan origination fees. You are on the earning side of the equation.

There are two types of people in this world; those that pay interest and those that earn it. Make sure you are on the earning side of the interest equation.

DAN KITCHEN

Donald Trump has practically become a household name. He's worth over $4 Billion and is a self-made real estate investor. He understands real estate. He is good at real estate. But do you ever see him hammering nails or ripping up carpet? You probably won't catch him changing a leaky toilet in the middle of the night either. He is the money man. He sees an opportunity and he puts his money to work. He has learned the art of leveraging other people's money and other people's opportunities.

Safety:

Bridge loans are extremely safe because there is a physical building acting as collateral. This isn't a paper asset or an idea. This is a REAL asset hence the name real estate. It doesn't get any more real than brick and mortar.

One of the main reasons for the dot-com bubble bursting was that it wasn't real. It was the internet and websites. It was digital ones and zeroes hubbed on a server. The same can be said of

Wall Street today. It is mostly smoke and mirrors. The stock market is rigged and is now being run by super computers. This isn't conspiracy theory. Very little trading happens with humans anymore. Now there are high frequency trading computers that can trade stocks in mere nano-seconds.

Surprise, the returns reported by mutual funds aren't actually earned by investors.

JACK BOGLE, founder of Vanguard

The financial institutions on Wall Street are even more secretive than the banks. They trade billions of dollars secretly each day in something called "Dark Pools". These dark pools allow institutions to trade large blocks of their own stocks completely off the radar and undetected by the rest of the market. As of 2014 these dark pools now make up 15% of all trades in the US. Billions of dollars are secretly traded here on a daily basis and your money is not allowed to play. Does it make you wonder what other secrets they are keeping from us?

With a bridge loan there is an office building, water-bottling plant, beachfront Hawaiian hotel or commercial space involved. A building you could actually drive to and place your hands on. A building that needs expansion, upgrades or new construction. A building that brings in money each month.

Every loan extended by the group, is done with a purpose. Every property has had two appraisals done to make sure the values are known before lending. Every property has the proper insurance in place in case of a fire or natural disaster. In addition to this, the group will never lend more than 65% of the value of the property. This is very important and we should let numbers tell the story.

Let's say for example that a $14 Million beach front property in Hawaii is seeking a $3 Million loan to remodel and upgrade their facility. This will keep cash flowing because tourists want a 'clean and new feeling' place to stay for a week or more. After doing 2 appraisals, checking credit and reviewing financial statements the group decides to extend the borrower a bridge loan. 6 months into the 12 month payback the hotel cannot make payments. They have paid back half the loan but the rest is outstanding and in default. If the hotel cannot meet their obligation the group will be forced to foreclose. If foreclosure occurs the group just picked up a $14 million hotel for $3 million. Even in a fire sale they could get $7 million out of the beach front property and walk away with a healthy profit.

Bridge loans are not designed to get out of this world returns. That isn't the kind of risk these loans are after. They are looking to get their clients a solid 5-7% return in a 12 month period. If the loan defaults, the group has reserve funds in place and contractually guarantees they will indemnify your principal.

So what does it mean to indemnify your investment? Let's say you invest $100,000 and you were able to lock in a 6% interest rate for 12 months. You would earn $6,000 which would be paid over 12 months. In this case $6,000 divided by 12 means you are earning and receiving $500 a month. So, if after 6 months the property defaulted and had to be foreclosed on, you have earned $3,000 in interest and your full $100,000 is released back to you and is available to go into another property or to a different investment.

Now I want to be clear. Foreclosing on bridge plans rarely happens, but it is important to know what happens in a worst-case scenario. This is why a real asset is important. When the stock market dropped by 38% in 2008, could you call the companies you owned stock in and ask for your money back? NO. Could you sue them for the money or other assets they own? Nope! You were simply out of luck and if you waited 5.5 years, your money would come back to break even. This represents wasted time and money.

In the event of default, most properties are either sold or refinanced with a bank until the project can be completed. For this reason foreclosures or defaults are extremely rare and this is why having a real asset to work with is so valuable.

Security:

Bridge plans use qualified escrow affiliates with experience in third party fund management. These fund custodians are under a microscope when it comes to managing funds. They are audited on a regular basis and in most cases are under SEC watch or their state banking commission. It is wise to work only with companies that use a reputable third party account fund managers. Most companies will have excellent reputations and can be checked with the better business bureau.

With a Bridge Plan you will also be sent the property's appraisal and paperwork showing you are the first position lien holder on the loan. You will also know where the building is located. You can drive there if you like. Check with your accountant because you may be able to write off a trip to visit your property. I for one like the idea of owning property in California so I can write off my trip while I visit the state.

The last thing I want to point out is the security that comes from having a real building as the asset backing your money. Remember when the US Dollar was backed by gold in Fort Knox? We had a gold reserve fund. We were the most powerful country in the world. Our currency became the reserve currency of the world. Then our country went off the gold standard. Money was now just paper and faith. It is only worth what someone is willing to trade for it. This sounds like the stock market.

Having an income producing property backing your money makes this investment real and makes it real safe.

No Management Fees:

There are no management fees or ongoing percentage cuts for managing your investment. The group you invest with is compensated during the property acquisition phase and upon pay out just like the investors themselves. This means all money you allocate into a bridge plan participates in the investment. The group makes their money in the investment just like you and me.

If you invest $100,000, all $100,000 participates. In the event that qualified funds are used such as an IRA or 401k, there is an annual custodial fee of $100-$500, for paperwork and reporting to the IRS. This keeps fees from devouring your growth. Your bridge plan specialist will be able to provide you with the custodial fees on your account.

Having a fixed fee structure prevents erosion on earnings and principle. Paying a flat $250 per year regardless of having a $25,000 or a $25,000,000 investment, ensures that you aren't being taken advantage of by fees.

Liquidity:

Although bridge plans are not a liquid investment like a savings or checking account, the investment time frame is typically 12 months. On occasion an 18-24 month opportunity will present itself but you, as the client, choose the contracts you wish to participate in. At no time will the group choose for you.

Upon completion of a contract, investors may move their funds if they so choose. This is a good investment for retirement dollars that have time to grow and season because it allows the client to truly compound their money year after year. It also allows you to receive monthly interest to live on if necessary or the ability to walk away after 12 months if desired. Flexibility and short time frames are imperative for smart investing. You want steady growth and short durations.

In the case of IRA accounts or old 401Ks, investors will need to be mindful of the Required Minimum Distributions that begin at age 70 1/2. With a bridge plan you don't have to time the market or have your investment end at just the right time. You have monthly liquid interest payments to make the required minimum distributions and full release of principal at the end of your term.

Clear Exit Strategy:

One of the most difficult aspects of investing in the stock market is timing the market; knowing when to sell and when to hold out further.

With a bridge plan, you do not have to time anything. Your principal is protected and you will know from day one what the time frame is on each property.

Most contracts have a time frame of 12 months. You will decide which contracts to purchase. Your specialist will help you determine which contracts are best, depending on your time frame and goals.

Easy to Understand:

Bridge plans are easy to understand and so is the math. You are lending money on an income generating property with a fixed time frame and a fixed rate of return.

The borrower is making a monthly payment to the group and the group is making a monthly interest payment to you. Most of us have had a car loan or home loans so this is easy to understand.

It is a win-win opportunity to help projects get completed, while placing yourself in a position to be on the earning side of the interest equation. Bridge plans are also valuable because they improve our economy, provide jobs and keep money from sitting stagnant at large corporations. Best of all, it feels good to earn interest like the banks.

Conclusion:

Bridge plans are a unique and safe way to grow your money. One of the largest industries in America is the real estate industry. Why do you suppose banks and lenders are willing to lend trillions of dollars to homeowners and businesses? Because there is a real asset backing the loan. There is a physical building that can be taken or repurposed or rented or sold off. Most bridge plans are only 12 months because after a project is completed and the appraisal shows the increased value, the project is sold for a profit or refinanced with a bank at a lower rate.

Participating in bridge plans is good for your money and your future money needs. It provides jobs and keeps the economy moving and growing.

Bridge plans aren't for everyone. They typically require $25,000 or more per property. Some investors would rather be hands-on and be their own source of capital for buying and flipping homes. More money can be made by doing it yourself, but the clients I have in the program are too busy working full-time to be renovating real estate. Bridge plans are for people that like real estate and see how much money there is to be made, but don't have the time, patience (that's me) or skill set to do it themselves. If done wrong you bear the full weight of the property and are solely responsible. There is power in numbers and collectively pooling your money with experienced investors. This is where our group excels.

If you like the idea of putting your capital to work in real assets and having it grow safely, then a bridge plan may be right for you. Our investors have enjoyed using an investment that is backed by a physical building. Your bridge plan specialist can help you compare this to other investments and returns. Your specialist can also help you control your fees and make sure your money is working for you. Bridge plans provide control and predictability and have a contract in place that dictates everyone's responsibilities and obligations and the guaranteed interest rate. This gives incredible peace of mind and allows clients to feel secure in the pursuit of their goals.

Chapter Eight
Become Self-Directed

You have to learn the rules of the game, and then you have to play better than anyone else.

ALBERT EINSTEIN

What if I told you there was a way to take control of your qualified money? Your IRA, Roth IRA, SEP IRA, Simple Plan, Solo K, Old 401K, Old 403B and the list goes on and on. What if you were your own money manager? What if you made the decisions on your money and cut out the middle man? Not only the middle man but the middle man's fees.

There is a tool that less than 5% of Americans know about. A tool that allows you to direct your own money and control your own destiny. It's called a self-directed IRA.

A self-directed IRA is a tool used by the wealthy to take control of their money and perform their own investments. All qualified plans can be converted to a self-directed status.

This tool has been buried and kept secret by the big investment houses and banks. Knowledge of these plans would take trillions of dollars away from Wall Street. It would block advisors from skimming money off your account. It would empower you too much and make many advisors obsolete. Wall Street and the banks don't want you to know about being self-directed. They don't want to lose control of you and your money.

We all live under the same sky, but we don't all have the same horizon.

CONRAD ADENAUER

One of the major benefits of being self-directed is being in charge of your own money. Do you think you would be more protective of your own money than someone else? Of course you would. No one cares about your money as much as you, except maybe the IRS!

Do you think you would do more personal research on an investment before pulling the trigger if you were solely responsible? Of course you would, you would have to. This will make you smarter and increase your understanding of money.

Don't be intimidated by this! There will be advisors and programs out there that will take time to help you fully understand how an investment works. They will show you how the money is made. They will help you understand the math and the potential risks and rewards.

> *The secret of change is to focus all of the energy, not on fighting the old, but on building the new.*

SOCRATES

As Americans have become busier and busier, they have outsourced their money and retirement planning to the point of not knowing how it all works or why their money is where it is. We've lost control and become dependent upon Wall Street for our future; the same people that took corporate bail out dollars to issue executive bonuses and organize extravagant vacations. All this, while leaving the American people hanging out to dry and wondering how so much of their money disappeared.

A Bridge plan allows individuals to use qualified funds like an IRA or old 401K to participate. Until a self-directed program became available, most people were stuck with the investments their advisor had to offer or that their company had selected for them. How many people have signed up for a company 401k with only a few funds to choose from and then taken investment advice from an HR employee that makes $15 an hour? It happens all the time! We are smarter than this, but we didn't know we had the option.

Another major reason to self-direct is to save on fees. Later in the fees chapter you will learn how many of my clients have saved thousands of dollars by cutting out the middle man and eliminating the annual percentage charges. These fees will eat your funds alive. Now you can cut your fees to less than a couple hundred dollars a year.

No advisor that makes his money for holding your money is ever going to recommend this strategy. It would take money out of his or her wallet and diminish his annual commissions.

No bank is going to educate you on how to be in charge of your own money or recommend better opportunities that take your cold, hard cash from their grasp. They don't like closing accounts or seeing money walk out the door, but then again you don't like being ripped off and under paid. Now you know there is a better way. I hope you will take it.

Ask your bridge plan specialist to discuss a self-directed IRA with you today. Take control of your money and keep more of it with lower fees and the freedom a self-directed IRA will give you.

Chapter Nine

Stick to the Contract

An investment operation is one which, upon thorough analysis, promises safety of principle and an adequate return. Operations not meeting this requirement are speculative.

BENJAMIN GRAHAM,

The Intelligent Investor

By this point, you're probably thinking this sounds amazing, but want to better understand how your money will contractually grow. Remember with a bridge plan we aren't using hope as a strategy. We are using a legally-binding contract that dictates your exact time commitment and guaranteed interest rate.

If you place $100,000 dollars and lock a 6% rate for 12 months you will earn $6,000 that year which will come to you each and every month. That's $500 a month, without any guesswork. This is the power of using contracts with real assets.

The point of living is to believe the best is yet to come.

PETER USTINOV

The only moving part in a bridge plan is the passage of time, so once a contract is purchased, and the contractual return is posted, the clock starts ticking. To figure out how your money will grow in a years' time, we multiply your money by 1 plus the interest rate. If you have a 5% rate you would times your money by 1.05 to see how your money will grow that year.

$$\$100,000 \times 1.05 = \$105,000$$

The beauty of a bridge plan is really understanding how the money will grow and having everything completed by contract versus speculation.

The tables below will give you an idea of how money will grow based on the contractually guaranteed rate. For this example, let's assume this is an IRA with a lump sum and no additional contributions.

5% Fixed Return

Years	Amount Invested	Annual Growth	Annual Return
1	$100,000	$105,000	5%
2	–	$110,250	5%
3	–	$115,762	5%
4	–	$121,550	5%
5	–	$127,628	5%

6% Fixed Return

Years	Amount Invested	Annual Growth	Annual Return
1	$100,000	$106,000	6%
2	–	$112,360	6%
3	–	$119,101	6%
4	–	$126,247	6%
5	–	$133,822	6%

7% *Fixed Return*

Years	Amount Invested	Annual Growth	Annual Return
1	$100,00	$107,000	7%
2	—	$114,490	7%
3	—	$122,504	7%
4	—	$131,079	7%
5	—	$140,255	7%

Knowing how your money will grow allows you to make plans for the future. It gives peace of mind to know where your money will be 5 or 10 years from now. You still have the option of gambling in the stock market and receiving whatever the market gives, good or bad. Or if you have idle money sitting at the bank, you could continue to leave it there to rot. Remember, you want to beat inflation without losing your money. If you can beat those two enemies of wealth you will have a bright future.

If you don't know where you are going, every road will get you there.

HENRY KISSINGER

I want to do one more comparison to help you understand how powerful this asset can be. Let's compare a bridge plan to traditional investments, with which you are most likely familiar. Let's assume you have $100,000 to save and you want to see how it will perform in a bridge plan contract versus the vehicles you've been familiar with your whole life.

The numbers used in the table below are the actual rates as of writing this book.

Account Type	Money placed	Growth rate	Amount at 5 years	Profit after 5 years
Savings	$100,000	.03% APR	$100,150	$150
CD	$100,000	1% APR	$105,124	$5,124
Bridge Plan	**$100,000**	**7% APR**	**$140,255**	**$40,255**
Stocks	$100,000	No Clue	No Clue	No Clue
Mutual Funds	$100,000	No Clue	No Clue	No Clue

As you can see from the chart, the savings vehicles offered by banks are sub-par and don't even keep up with inflation. Or as one of my clients put it, "I don't even make enough per year with our savings account to take my wife out to a nice dinner."

My wealth has come from a combination of living in America, some lucky genes, and compound interest.

WARREN BUFFETT

With stocks and mutual funds, the results are unclear and murky. Honestly ask yourself, where will your money be 5 years from now if you keep it in stocks and mutual funds? Who's to say it won't be less than what you have today? In 1999 and 2007, investors on Wall Street thought their money would just keep going up forever and ever. Their money was at an all-time high. However, after the market dropped, they spent the next 5 years scraping to get back to break even. Why lose? Why not secure contractual increases that are locked in from the moment you purchase?

Chapter Ten
Houston We Have a Fee Problem

The mutual fund industry is now the world's largest skimming operation, a $7 Trillion trough from which fund managers, brokers and the other insiders are steadily siphoning off an excessive slice of the nation's household, college and retirement savings.

SENATOR PETER FITZGERALD

When it comes to fees, bridge plans might be the most cost-effective investment around, except for that free checking account you opened in the 80s, when your local bank was handing out toasters. That was a pretty sweet deal!

In every single bridge plan conversation with a prospect or client, the question of fees has been brought up. Truth be told, I am usually the one bringing it up because it is such a great selling point for helping people truly compound their money without fees eating into their growth.

This chapter may be hard to read if you have money in the stock market or if you have money in an IRA or 401k. The reality is, you are being "fee'd" to death and don't even know it. Fees are quietly robbing you of your desired future.

That was the case with one of my clients in Illinois. Let's call him Mike, just to keep his real name anonymous. We had finished moving his money from TD Ameritrade over to his bridge plan investment account. Up to this point, Mike was very excited about the program. He had mentioned to me on several occasions how much sense this made to him and that he wished he had found it 20 years earlier.

A few weeks after wrapping up Mike's paperwork I was placing his folder in my filing cabinet when I accidentally dropped the file, exposing several of the pages from his former TD Ameritrade account.

Up to this point I had not noticed one of the pages. It was the small print page that discussed what Mike's fees were each year. I read the amount of $3,172.04 per year. I couldn't believe it. The fee on his bridge plan account was a flat $215 a year. Were we really saving him nearly $3,000 a year in fees? This made me wonder whether I was reading this incorrectly.

I phoned Mike to tell him about the fees I had uncovered on his former fund custodian's paperwork. When I told him the amount, Mike said, "You're kidding me, Steve." I wish I had been. Imagine if Mike had gone another 10 years, growing his money with this group, without knowing he was paying thousands of dollars in fees per year.

I will share one more story with you about another client of mine. Let's call him Dr. Markson for this story. My client is a fertility specialist and a really good one at that. As the doctor and I discussed his financial situation, he told me of the unfortunate losses his retirement account had suffered in 2008. He had lost 50% of his portfolio after his advisor kept telling him to wait it out.

The doctor shared his concerns about further losses and his decision to shift over to safer strategies. I couldn't blame him for being cautious. In fact, I still think he made the right decision to shift his account to a money market account.

However, this decision brought with it, low to non-existent interest rates. His account simply wasn't growing. You can't get far earning .1% on your money.

We had to have a long discussion on inflation and places to grow his money outside of Wall Street. At this point, the doctor had lost all confidence in the Wall Street casino. This is when we discussed putting a portion of his funds into a bridge plan.

This brought us to the discussion of fees. At first the doctor protested that he was not paying any fees. After all, he had never received an invoice or seen a charge on his credit card. I explained to him how the investment company skims the money off the account after crediting his earnings. He could hardly believe a well-known investment group would do such a thing.

The doctor called his investment group to request that his account fees and expenses be disclosed to him. After learning that he was being charged more than $15,000 a year in management fees, he was upset. Actually, he was furious and felt taken advantage of. No wonder his account value had not been growing. He then said, "Imagine if I had never known Steve. I would have paid them hundreds of thousands of dollars in fees over the course of my time with them."

Then I asked the doctor a question, which may have been poorly timed, but was important nonetheless. I asked, "What has the group done for you this year to deserve a $15,000 fee?"

"Nothing! They have done nothing for me. My account certainly didn't grow by that amount."

I then asked, "During that difficult time in 2008, when you lost nearly half of your hard earned money, did they take their fee while your account was losing?"

He replied, "Yes, they did take their fee, although it seems a little criminal."

I can't imagine losing any of my clients' money. I always recommend strategies that are safe and have safety precautions built-in to guard against loss. But on the crazy chance that I might lose someone's money, I can't imagine being able to charge their account an exorbitant fee and then look myself in the mirror.

If a restaurant botches your order, they don't charge you. If the dry cleaner ruins your shirt, they buy you a new shirt. If a valet company wrecks your car, their insurance will replace or fix the damages. But on Wall Street when they lose trillions of dollars of their clients' money, Wall Street still takes their fee and they still issue executive bonuses. It makes me sick!

A former CEO of the Vanguard group had this to say about fees: "What happens in the fund business is that the magic of compounding returns is overwhelmed by the tyranny of compounding costs."

He then continues with a great example of how these seemingly small fees can cut your money in half.

In an interview with John Bogle, Founder and former CEO of Vanguard:

"Okay, let's assume there are two investors: Investor No. 1 owns a portfolio of stocks worth $100,000, pays no ongoing fees (apart from commissions when he purchased his shares) and earns the market return of 7 percent annually. Investor No. 2 owns the same stocks in a mutual fund that charges 2 percent in fees and he therefore earns a return of 5 percent."

"Now fire up your compounding calculator, because the fun is about to begin. For Investor No. 1, in the box labeled "current principal," enter $100,000. Leave the next box, labeled "annual addition," blank, because we'll assume he doesn't make any additional contributions."

"Now, in the "years to grow" box, enter 50, and for "interest rate," enter 7. In the next box, make sure the calculator is set to "compound interest 1 time(s) annually." Finally, hit "calculate."

"If you've done everything right, you should see a "future value" of $2,945,702.51. This is what Investor No. 1 would end up with after 50 years at a growth rate of 7 per cent. To figure out his return, subtract the original $100,000, which gives you $2,845,702.51."

"Now do the same for Investor No. 2. The only number you need to change is the interest rate, which is now 5 per cent. Hit "calculate," and you'll get a future value of $1,146,739.98, for a return of $1,046,739.98."

"You'll notice that Investor No. 2's return is less than half of Investor No. 1's. In fact, consistent with Mr. Bogle's example, Investor No. 2 made about 63% less than Investor No. 1 – and all because of just 2% in fees charged every year."

As you can see, these ongoing management fees can devour your earnings over time. This is because the management fee hits your entire portfolio and new earnings every single year. So as you earn more and your money hopefully compounds, so do your management fees.

There are 17 hidden fees in 401Ks and nearly 20 hidden fees in mutual funds. So how will your money grow over the next 5 to 10 years? With the stock market you never know. You can only speculate and guess. Nothing is contractual. The only thing the big investment houses will put in a contract, is how much they will charge you to manage your money, whether it gains or loses and even that is buried or hidden most of the time.

I think the real sting of fees comes from discovering just how much they really are. Most of the people I have helped to uncover their fees are upset to realize how much they have been spending on annual fees. It appears what hurts the most is how they feel lied to, or tricked, or purposely kept in the dark. Sometimes you can forgive the wrong, but the lying about the wrong doing is the hardest part to overcome.

This happened with a gentleman in Virginia with whom I was working on a bridge plan. We went over these same undisclosed fees and he told me how grateful he was to not be one of the people fooled by fees. I was a little suspect when he told me he wasn't being charged fees. It wasn't that I didn't want to believe him. It's just that I am told that on a weekly basis; then I am the one left bearing the bad news. Don't shoot the messenger!

I decided not to push the issue as it seemed he was eager to get involved in the bridge plan program. However, about a week later I received an email which was filled with heated words and a sense of urgency to move his money ASAP.

This gentleman had just received his annual statement. He found the fee section of his plan. This gentleman was being charged one of the highest fees I had seen in all my years.

The fees listed as following on his statement:

Supplement dated March 29th, 2014
Of the Class A shares Prospectus dates
January 31st, 2014

Management Fee	1.50%
Distribution 12b-1 Fee	0.00%
Other expenses	0.62%
AFFE Fee	1.42%
Total Annual Fee	3.54%

So how do these small fees really affect your retirement funds growth? Let's say you had $100,000. Let's compare how 1%, 2% and 3% management fees look on your account. Let's also assume your account grows by 5%.

Starting balance	Interest rate earned	Interest Rate after Fees	Annual Percentage Fees
$100,000	5%	4%	1%
$100,000	5%	3%	2%
$100,000	5%	2%	3%

You can see very quickly, how the percent you earn is quickly diluted by the fees you must pay, but it gets worse because you aren't paying the fees on just the earnings. You are paying fees on the total amount managed. The tables below show you how fees eat into the growth on your account.

1% Annual Management Fee

Account balance	5% Return	1% fee	4% net return
$100,000	$5000	-$1050	$103,950

2% Annual Management Fee

Account balance	5% Return	2% fee	3% net return
$100,000	$5000	-$2100	$102,900

3% Annual Management Fee

Account balance	5% Return	3% fee	2% net return
$100,000	$5000	-$3150	$101,850

You can now see the tyranny of compounding fees as described by John Bogle. Your fund's custodian will place on your statement or verbally confirm that you have received a 5% increase for the year. The funds custodian will then subtract their annual management fee. This happens whether your account increases or decreases.

Can you see why Americans have less money than they should? Can you see why the creator of the 401K said that an annual management fee of just 1% over an employee's career could rob their retirement account of nearly 50%?

The math doesn't lie! This is why the numbers are well guarded and the conversation of fees is avoided at all costs. Let's look at the math just one other way to really drive home how much Wall Street is draining away from your account into theirs. In the case of the 1% fee above, the account earned $5,000 and the fee was $1,050. If we take the $1,050 divided by the $5,000 the calculator will show 21%.

This means that the annual management fee ate 21% of your annual return. With the 2% fee $2,100 divided by $5,000 is 42% of your earnings. With the 3% fee of $3,150 divide by $5,000 it is a whopping 63% of your total earnings for the year.

Wall Street is eating your growth for breakfast, lunch and dinner. Up until today, you may have never considered this. They take none of the risk, put up none of the money and keep the lion's share of the profits for themselves. To me this seems like a systemic issue the average investor will never win against.

I see very little appeal to earning 5-7% in the stock market only to have the big brokerage houses take 1-3% off the top. It leaves investors shouldering all of the market risk and getting less than they should. Why not have a legally-binding contract that dictates exactly what you will earn, doesn't have sneaky fees being taken off the top and is backed by a real asset?

If you get nothing else from this book and a bridge plan isn't right for you, at least be aware of how fees may destroy your future. You have the power to control this. I hope this information empowers you.

With a bridge plan you pay no fees on a cash investment and only $215 a year for IRA or old

401K funds. And in case you are wondering how your bridge plan specialist is compensated, they are paid a one-time referral fee when you buy into a property. No hidden fees!

This means if you lock in a 6% rate, you get the full amount credited to you. You also don't have any front-loading fees or commissions that eat into your principal. Your full principal amount participates. If you place $25,000, all $25,000 participates. If you place one million, your full one million participates.

Don't allow fees to rob you of the money you should have during the accumulation phase of your career and certainly don't allow fees to rob you of the growth and income you will need during your retirement years. You only get one shot at building your nest egg. Control your costs and look for contractual increases on your money. No more speculating or hoping for the retirement of your dreams. With a bridge plan you have peace of mind that fees aren't eating into your hard-earned money and aren't slowing down your growth.

Chapter Eleven
Christine and Jeff's Story

Give yourself peace of mind. You deserve to be happy. You deserve delight.

HANNAH ARENDT

As the financial world seemed to be crumbling, Christine and Jeff's world was just heating up. Neither of them could believe how the market dropping by over 30% in 2001 could serve as the lesson they needed to invest more wisely with their money during the 2008 market crash.

Christine is a successful member of the Mary Kay family; one of those fabulous and fierce women that drives the big pink Escalade around town. She is successful and runs a large team that empowers women to help each other and create income for their families. She loves what she does and has been doing it for over 20 years.

Jeff works for a large software company just outside of Washington DC as a manager. He's a self-described geek that loves to build websites and sequel database platforms for large companies. He's been with his current group for about 10 years now.

With Christine being self-employed, she had always placed her money with a money manager and Jeff had always participated in his company 401k. Both were good savers, but both were very busy and neither enjoyed investing much. So they left it up to more capable people.

2000-2001 was a rough year for Christine and Jeff. They lost over 30% in their retirement accounts thanks to the dot-com bubble and the 9/11 crisis. Because of Christine's training she had been taught to look for a lesson in everything and keep a positive attitude. However, she and Jeff decided they would never go through that again. They made a promise to each other that if the markets ever looked rocky again they would pull out and take a break.

Several years went by and the couple continued to save and let their money come back to break even. It took longer than they had hoped but it did come back around 2004. This was right about the time the market really started to heat up. The economy was doing well and so were they. Christine's team had grown like crazy as more and more women saw the incredible opportunity Mary Kay gave them. Jeff had taken a new job and had started a new 401k.

He let the old 401k sit at his past employer until one day a friend at church told him about a self-directed IRA he was using. Jeff had no clue what a self-directed IRA was but he liked the idea of being in charge of his money. He hadn't done anything with that money for almost 2 years because he hadn't come across any programs he liked and he didn't have time to research like he wanted to before feeling confident.

One day Jeff got a letter in the mail that described a new way of investing in real estate. A way to do hard money lending with a group of investors on commercial properties through a program called a bridge plan. He and Christine met with Mark, the specialist that had sent them the letter. Within 10 minutes the investment made sense to him. Christine didn't know much about real estate but she knew that some of the more successful ladies at Mary Kay were involved in real estate so she remained open to the idea.

After a couple weeks of doing their research and learning about the companies involved, they decided to test Jeff's old 401k with around $80,000. They first bought into a golf course in Georgia that wanted to expand their club house. It was a 12 month contract and would pay them 8% interest. They liked that they didn't have to do any of the work or fly to Georgia to supervise. They had a legally-binding contract in place and the golf course was used as collateral on the loan. At the end of the 12 month term, Jeff and Christine were happy with how the investment had grown and with the increase they had received on their money.

At this time, many of their friends were buying and flipping real estate. They were bragging about making 15-20% returns and flipping houses every 6 months. It seemed the market was only getting hotter and so Jeff pulled his money out to invest with his friends. The money was good and it seemed almost too easy. Eventually Jeff's money just sat because it was cheaper to borrow from the bank.

Around the middle of 2007 the housing market was in full swing. Investors were tripping over opportunities and making money left and right. It seemed there was no end in sight. Jeff even considered quitting his software job because he could make so much more. Luckily Christine wouldn't let him. She felt uneasy about the whole thing and worried they would be left holding the bag.

By summer, Christine had a feeling that something was about to shift in the economy. Several of the women in her Mary Kay family had complained that their husbands had been laid off or that work was slowing down. That night Christine sat Jeff down to discuss her uneasy feelings. She reminded Jeff of the major blow they had been dealt with the economy dropping and the stock markets losing. Jeff was the first to bring up the promise they had made to each other in 2001.

About a week later Jeff and Christine decided to sell all their real estate investment properties and see what the market would do. They moved their money over to a money market account that was earning 4% at the time. By late 2007 the housing and construction markets had come to a screeching halt. Housing had hit the top of the market and was starting its descent quickly.

They watched friend after friend struggle to sell off their properties. They watched as loved ones were laid off. They sat and listened as family complained of losses in their retirement account. Some of them had lost over 50% of their money. They felt lucky that they had learned from 2001 and taken action. Then the great recession hit full-swing. Jeff was laid off and the Mary Kay business slowed down. Jeff was able to find another job quickly but at lower pay.

By 2009 their money market account was earning less than 1%. They decided that if interest rates were going to be low, they would focus on paying down credit card debt. They took a Dave Ramsey course on how to pay off their debt fast.

It was a finance course taught over several weeks and they enjoyed learning about money and how to get out of debt together. On the last night of the course, the instructor spoke to the group about inflation and the rule of 72. They had never heard of the rule of 72 and had no idea about inflation. They had heard the word, but hadn't paid attention.

Part of their homework that night was to run their interest rates against 72 to see how often their money would double. They started with their money market account. They hadn't noticed that it was only earning .3%. They ran the calculation and it came back at 240 years. That couldn't be right. They ran it again. Christine joked that in 240 years not even their great grandchildren would be alive. Heck, the United States of America was not even 240 years old. This had to change.

Once a week, Christine and Jeff would set aside an hour to do research and read about investing. They knew they needed to do something but didn't know what to do. All they could find with their investment advisor was low-earning products or mutual funds.

They kept searching. Real estate had been good to them but now prices were low and no one could get financing. They didn't want to take on the risk of buying and flipping properties and frankly, they didn't have the time or energy for it.

One night in 2010, Christine and Jeff reviewed what investments they had done in the past that were easier and didn't involve a lot of risk. He mentioned the bridge plans had been easy and didn't involve a lot of time. He again reached out to Mark, the specialist that had first introduced him to the concept. Mark was still in business and was still helping people put their money to work with bridge plans and other safe investments.

Jeff asked if there was still an opportunity for Christine and him to be involved. Mark said that there was but that things had changed a little. During 2007 and 2008 the investment group had not lost anyone's money but they had made a lot of changes to their lending practices. The group had become more conservative and particular with whom they would lend money. Their appetite for risk was much lower. They were now only lending up to 65% of the property value, the borrowers couldn't have any other liens or obligations on the property and the interest rates were lower. Instead of the 7-9% they were now 5-7%.

Jeff laughed and told Mark he would be very happy with a 5% return right now. He told Mark how his money market account was only earning .3%. The next week Mark, Jeff and Christine got on the computer together and looked at available properties. Before they had had dozens of properties to choose from, now they had only 3-4. Jeff and Christine were grateful the group was being extra-cautious.

They ended up placing Jeff's old 401K and Christine's money into a couple of properties. One was a hotel in Texas and the other, a commercial office building in Baltimore. They even picked up a rental property in Beverly Hills, California. They liked that the group promised a contractual return and agreed to indemnify them out of their reserve account if the property had issues down the road. They also liked that the time frame was only 12 months long. They wanted something flexible but they also wanted something real to be backing their money.

Money is a good servant, but a bad master.

SIR FRANCIS BACON

Now 4 years later, they are very happy with the investment. They have averaged 6% and haven't had any interruptions in their interest payments. This has allowed both Christine and Jeff to focus on their jobs and family. The group has always had another good property ready to roll into as their 12 month term was ending. They've even invited several of their family and friends to be involved.

Christine and Jeff are dedicated to protecting and growing their money and the bridge plan has been an incredible tool with which to do so.

.

Chapter Twelve
Plan For a Peaceful Future

Make it a must that whenever you hear about something, read or research something you think has value for your life, don't let it become knowledge. Convert it into action, for it is through actions that our destiny is shaped.

TONY ROBBINS

One of the most satisfying experiences of my career has been calling clients to tell them their 12 months are up and it's time to select another property. To tell them their accounts will continue to safely compound interest for another year. For clients to hear that their account value is growing just as we discussed when they first came on board is exciting.

Another satisfying aspect of what I do has come from getting phone calls during distressing times when the stock market has dropped and being able to reassure a client that their money has not dropped in value.

Wealth is the ability to fully experience life.

HENRY DAVID THOREAU

I remember one such call that came in the fall of 2013. The US government had been shut down for over 10 days. The stock market was dropping and the evening news was reporting about how our country might possibly default on payments to China. It was a scary time.

My client called to make sure his account was safe. He reminded me that I had told him that if the markets dropped, his account would be safe. He reminded me that when the stock market dropped by $300 billion in 2011 after the earthquake in Japan that I said no one had lost money in their bridge plan account.

I could tell he was scared because his portfolio had lost over 40% in 2008 with a former advisor, and he was not looking forward to receiving bad news again. We got on the computer together and looked up his account. While we were pulling up his account, I reminded him that his money was not in the stock market and his earnings were not linked to the performance or health of the economy, the jobs report or the consumer confidence report.

I reminded my client that his funds were backed by an income producing building that he had fractional ownership in. A building that he could go visit if he wanted. We discussed how the group would never make a loan of more than 65% of what the building had appraised for. This protects investors from falling property values. This seemed to jog his memory and put him at ease. Still, I pulled up his account so we could look at it together.

The account pulled up and my client could see that his money was all there. He could see that, although the stock market had dropped, his account value had not. We then looked over his contracts, the time frame and how they would grow contractually. He could see that his interest payments had come on time every month and a few days prior his most recent interest check had arrived.

This gave my client peace of mind. He told me how he had started to relive 2008. Seeing the stock market drop had conjured up all the stress and fear he had felt back then. It made me feel good to know that my client had protected his money and that he knew how it would grow. I look forward to calling this particular client in the near future to tell him that we've completed another 12 month bridge loan and it is time to be on the lookout for another property.

The secret of getting ahead is getting started.

MARK TWAIN

I have tremendous peace of mind knowing that my clients have money inside of investments they can understand. Knowing how their investments work is empowering and crucial for success. Having a real asset backing your investments is also important. I hope this book has given you an understanding of how this powerful asset class works. I know this strategy is not for everyone and not everyone will qualify to use it, but the clients that have moved forward with our team have been very happy they did.

So where do you go from here?

I believe you owe it to yourself to better understand how this asset can benefit your retirement, your peace of mind and your future. You have nothing to lose by learning more about bridge plans and peace of mind and interest to gain. You must beat inflation and for now, that means leaving the banks. You must also avoid losses like the plague and that means shifting funds away from the volatility of Wall Street.

Most of the companies I have relationships with are willing to educate you on their process and show you the contracts they have available. In fact, with most you can see dollar for dollar how your money will contractually increase before you ever sign any papers or place a single dime in a property. Very few investments can show you a glimpse of your future, even fewer can give you the peace of mind that it will come to fruition.

The most difficult thing is the decision to act, the rest is merely tenacity.

AMELIA EARHART

See how your money will grow. Better understand why the largest banks, investment groups and hedge funds are using bridge plans. Better understand how they are using it with the money they are not willing to risk in the market and how it balances out their portfolio. There are huge advantages to real estate, with the biggest being the fact that it is real and tangible.

See for yourself and your family how this could be a huge stress reliever. Free up the time you used to spend watching MSNBC and Cramer trying to guess what the next hot stock will be; or the time you spend on Yahoo finance looking for P/E ratios and undervalued stocks. Free your mind from the frustration of opening your bank statements each month only to see that your earnings are grossly disappointing.

Remember that a rising tide lifts all boats and a lowering tide reveals who has been swimming naked. With the Federal Reserve printing billions of dollars every month to place in the stock market, we are seeing a rising tide, albeit an artificial rising of the tide. The market WILL drop again. History has proven it time and time again. The tides are sinking. Don't get caught naked!

Warning!

It is human nature when we first hear about a new concept that resonates with us to first imagine how this could benefit us or someone we care about.

The second reaction is to go back to our normal routine or to what we feel is most comfortable. This is natural, but not necessarily good. If you are reading this book it is because you have probably suffered retirement account losses in the past and you want a better way of growing your money than the banks have to offer. Doing what was considered traditional or accepted by the masses is what got most of us in trouble in the first place.

You can choose not to let the bank abuse you. You can choose to learn and become familiar with a bridge plan. You can choose to protect and grow your money away from the high fees of Wall Street. You can earn good returns without all the risk. You can't control the market, but with the right tools and information you can make smart and profitable decisions for your future. You can take control!

Peace of mind

What is it you are really trying to accomplish with your investments? Surely you want peace of mind. You want to know with certainty that you will be able to retire or if already retired, that you won't run out of money. You want to know that you won't lose money again. You want to be able to dream and make plans for your future.

Riches are not an end of life, but an instrument of life.

HENRY WARD BEECHER

Investing in the stock market has made peace of mind next to impossible. The stock market has robbed more Americans of their dreams than any other thing. It doesn't have to be this way. You can control your future and you can invest in predictable assets.

Bridge plans provide peace of mind to investors, proving that they can grow their money contractually. Having a contract in place that dictates how your money will grow should be a requirement of all investments. Would you take a new job and work for a year, not knowing what you would be paid? No contractor breaks ground on a new building without knowing their client can pay them and how much they will be paid. Having a contract in place is a sound business practice.

A journey of a thousand miles begins with a single step.

LAO TZU

Let our group design for you a peace of mind blueprint; a financial blueprint that ends with you having your money safe and growing and which takes away the worry of guessing whether the market will crash this month or next. Take away the speculation and walk away from the gambling. Wall Street and casinos are set up to make sure the house wins, no matter how many people have to lose to make it happen.

Let us answer your questions about bridge plans. Let us show you the value of this asset class.

Let us show you how your money will grow and the peace of mind that comes from not having to worry, or dwell a single second more on what the stock market is doing. Let us show you how to beat the banks and inflation. Let us show you how to put your money to work in a real asset that provides real growth to your nest egg.

Begin your peace of mind planning by working with the agent or advisor who gave you this book. If it was given to you, it's because the agent felt this strategy would be a good fit for your financial situation.

Giving this book to you says something about the agent you are working with, too. They are most likely well-read and continually educating themselves for their client's benefit. Start by asking how this strategy could benefit your personal situation. Then let them explain the ins and outs of a truly unique asset.

Finally, take the next step and see how the contracts and properties available will safely and contractually grow your money. Let this win-win investment safely carry you to your retirement dreams and bridge the gap between where you are now and where you want to be.

ACKNOWLEDGMENTS

I have always been interested in real estate and have personally seen the wealth that can be made from this real asset. Over the years I have run into many people, that like me, wanted to participate in real estate, but didn't have the time required to do it well. Bridge Plans allow me and my clients to have fractional ownership for a brief moment in time of some of the best commercial real estate in America.

It's not easy running a national, multi-million dollar company and still finding time to write a book. I want to thank all of the people who have brought me to this point in my life. This is my fourth book and your support has made this possible and enjoyable. I hope this book will have a huge impact on the way people look at their precious retirement dollars. I hope it will increase their understanding of ways to save outside of mainstream methods.

I want to thank my wife Kacey for being my greatest supporter. Your encouragement and support have been vital to my success. You have stood by me through good times and bad. You have championed me to stretch and be the best version of myself. The saying that 'behind every good man is an even better woman' is most definitely true with you. Thank you.

Thank you to my children who are the reasons for working as hard as I do. I hope to not only be a strong support for you to lean on in life, but to arm you with the necessary information that you will need to be successful in life.

Thank you to my parents who have raised me up right and who have taught me good financial principles, since I was a child. Thank you for giving me independence and support throughout my whole life. Thank you for encouraging me to be a lifelong learner and seeing me for who I would become.

Thank you to my sister Gretchen who proudly shares everything I create and supports me and my family.

Thank you, Mark Maiewski, for inspiring me. Your insight and wisdom is invaluable. Thank you, thank you, thank you!

Thank you Ron Weller, Ken Feyer, Paul Johnson and Morgen Jackson for all of your help.

A special thanks to Jeff Hays for all of his support over the past decade. Thank you to Julie Anderson and her wonderful parents for always loving and supporting me.

ABOUT THE AUTHOR

Stephen Gardner is a safe money specialist that lives in Salt Lake City, Utah with his wife and 3 children. He is also a national sales trainer and speaker in the financial services industry. He has often been heard saying "I am on a mission to strengthen America one family at a time." He is passionate about helping families get safe returns on their retirement funds. Although he calls himself Stephen, many of his clients and friends call him Safe Money Steve.

Stephen is also the founder of the Safe Millionaire Club and the best-selling author of The Billion Dollar Blueprint and the Smartest Doctor in the Room.

Request a personalized Blueprint:

Work with the author directly or one of his Bridge Plan specialists from all over the country.

To get a personalized blueprint today and see how your money will grow and be protected. Contact our office today to schedule a time for us to speak. Let us show you a safer way to achieve your financial goals.

Contact us:

Stephen@YourBridgePlan.com

888-638-0080.

To learn more about Bridge Plans and how they can help you beat inflation and earn solid returns with real assets, visit our website at:

YourBridgePlan.com

Additional Resources

Videos to help explain Bridge Plans

www.yourbridgeplan.com/videos

To work with the author

www.yourbridgeplan.com/contact

41503427R00080

Made in the USA
Lexington, KY
15 May 2015